This journal belongs to:

....

NATIONAL
GEOGRAPHIC
KiDS

dream
journal

Uncover the Power of Your Dreams
and the Science of Sleep With Dr. Allan Peterkin

NATIONAL GEOGRAPHIC
WASHINGTON, D.C.

introduction

Why I Wrote This Book

I love dreaming. My days are filled with facts, decisions, and chores. But at night, in my dreams, my magical mind roams free of the limits—like gravity or deadlines—that shape our waking hours.

As a doctor, I know the importance of good sleep for maintaining both physical and mental health. Yet our lives are becoming ruled by smartphones and other devices that distract us and intrude on our slumber. No wonder so many of us are sleep—and dream—deprived! Yet when we ARE able to drift off to dreamland, we can learn from our dreams and even use some of the messages we find in them to make important life changes.

The medical professor part of me is excited by the scientific advances we are making in understanding the brain's many complex functions. But as a writer, I like that we will never fully understand all of the mysteries of the human mind and imagination, especially dreams. Because even though the average brain weighs only three pounds (1.4 kg), its cells make some 100 trillion connections—that's right, 100,000,000,000,000! Dreams give us a fascinating glimpse into where those connections can lead.

I hope that the tips and exercises in this book make you more curious about your dreams and how they make you the one-of-a-kind person that you are!

—Dr. Allan Peterkin

how to use your dream journal

Have you ever dreamed of flying? Or being chased by a monster? Or showing up to class to discover there's a test you didn't know about?

Your brain has the amazing ability to conjure up weird, colorful images; terrific sounds; ultracomplicated plots; and—sometimes—everyday worries. In our dreams, we're free to explore and find solutions without the limits of time, logic, space, or any other real-world rules. If you think your newest app or video game is totally awesome, it has nothing on your dreams. Dreams somehow seem to create an incredible virtual reality model of the world. That model is updated with cool new content several times each night, every night of the week!

Even though you do dream every night, you may have times when you think your dreams took a night off because you can't remember anything when you wake up. We're here to help! In this journal, you'll find dozens of exercises to help you rev up, remember, and interpret your own dreams. You'll learn about the history and science of dreaming. You'll even read different ideas about what those nighttime stories mean. As you have fun exploring this book, you'll learn a lot about yourself, AND you'll create a supercool record of your own spectacular dreams!

> You can't dream big if you don't get some deep sleep. Use the terrific tips on page 52 to sleep well and dream even better!

Getting Started

If you want to write about dreams, first you have to pay attention to them. Before you go to sleep, keep telling yourself that you really want to remember what goes on in your dreams. When you wake up, start with the big picture, and then try to recall the details bit by bit. Keep your mind open to whatever plays out, no matter how weird it all seems once you are awake.

This book will help you dive deeper and deeper into your unique dream world. Each journal page has a prompt to help kick-start your writing. Feel free to use the prompt—or ignore it completely! It's up to you. You might notice that some of the prompts appear more than once, so you can use the same prompt to explore the significance of different dreams.

You can read this journal from front to back or jump around among the different sections of the book. As you go, look for these icons:

 History & Culture

 Science of Sleep

 Try This!

If a Try This! activity involves waking yourself up from sleep, be sure to try it on a weekend or another night when it doesn't matter as much that you'll be interrupting your sleep. Talk with your family before you try an exercise, so they know what you have in mind.

Fill in the journal in any order that inspires you to create a fantastic log full of your one-of-a-kind nighttime stories!

dream journal

in your dreams

Generally, people have three types of dreams:

Dreams based on real life. These dreams replay events that actually happened or create a made-up story line with real people, places, and situations.

Fantastic dreams. These can seem like they have nothing to do with reality. They're full of weird, over-the-top scenes like flying or morphing into someone—or something—else. They break all the rules and can blend together stories of the past, present, and future.

Nightmares. These dreams contain creepy or upsetting content that makes us nervous when we wake up. They are common, frequent, and may replay troubling situations that happened in the past.

Kids around age five generally have simple dreams featuring animals and people, but not themselves. Around age seven, kids start showing up as characters in their own dreams.

depositing dreams in your memory bank

Did you know that many of our dreams mirror our everyday routines? So they don't stand out. (They get deleted from your memory like spam on your computer.) But those weird, wacky, fantastic dreams sure do! You're most likely to remember those intense dreams, especially if you wake up while you're dreaming. In fact, studies show that people who woke up easily, woke up more often during the night, or were more alert to their surroundings while sleeping were most likely to remember their dreams.

As the night progresses, our dreams get more detailed and last longer—about 30 to 45 minutes, compared to 5 to 10 minutes at the very start of the night. Those longer dreams have a richer story and are full of details that are fresher in our minds when we wake up—that's why we are much more likely to remember those later dreams.

> If you wake up during your dream, pay attention to where you are in your bed. That may be your primo dream-catching position!

Try talking about your dreams with friends and family. Not only can it be fun, but it can also spark more memories and images from your dreams. And if a particular dream upsets you, they might be able to help you figure it out.

Tips for Remembering Dreams

1. Before you go to bed, start telling yourself that you want to have a good dream. Be specific. You might tell yourself, "I want to fly tonight!" or "I want to explore space!" Sometimes, the power of suggestion can actually work! (And don't forget to tell yourself that you WILL remember your dreams.)

2. When you wake up, notice how you are feeling. Happy? Sad? Scared? Before you get out of bed, take a deep breath. Keep your eyes closed and allow images, sounds, and words from your dreams to bubble up. Keep still and don't force it. Let the process happen naturally.

3. Keep this journal by your bedside so you can write as you wake up. Take your time. Often, just one detail or image can help flesh out an entire story or help you remember the rest of your dream. Using your journal daily will help you figure out what makes you tick.

Date:

Describe your dream. What thoughts and feelings did you
have when you first woke up? What thoughts and feelings
do you have when you think about your dream now? If you
were to choose an emoji to represent how your dream
made you feel, what would it be?

Date:

Describe what happened in your dream in as few sentences as possible. Just note the basic facts: beginning, middle, and end.
   Now try to fill in the details. What did the dream look like? What did it sound like?

Date:

Think about last night's dream. What did you like about it, if anything? If you could dream about anything, what would it be?

....

....

....

....

....

....

....

....

....

....

....

....

SCIENCE OF SLEEP **Z**

How Much Sleep Do We Really Need?

You can't dream if you don't sleep! According to the National Sleep Foundation, here's how much sleep most people need:

- Schoolkids (6–13), 9–11 hours
- Teenagers (14–17), 8–10 hours
- Young adults (18–25), 7–9 hours
- Adults (26–64), 7–9 hours
- Older adults (65+), 7–8 hours

Date:

A setting is where something takes place. What was the setting in your most recent dream? If it was somewhere familiar, what are your associations with or memories of that place?

Name a connection between your dream and things that are happening in your life right now.

Kids older than age nine remember their dreams more often than adults do.

Tree-mendous Dreams

Sometimes you can remember only one word or one picture from a dream. Use that one item to create a word association tree.

TRY THIS!

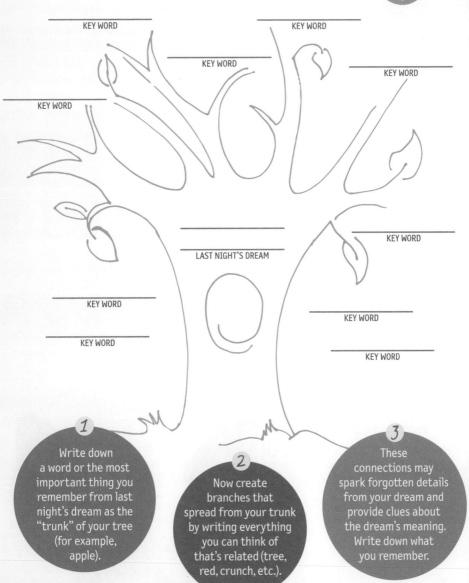

KEY WORD

KEY WORD

KEY WORD

KEY WORD

KEY WORD

KEY WORD

LAST NIGHT'S DREAM

KEY WORD

KEY WORD

KEY WORD

KEY WORD

1
Write down a word or the most important thing you remember from last night's dream as the "trunk" of your tree (for example, apple).

2
Now create branches that spread from your trunk by writing everything you can think of that's related (tree, red, crunch, etc.).

3
These connections may spark forgotten details from your dream and provide clues about the dream's meaning. Write down what you remember.

Date:

Did your dream last night make a lot of sense? Did it help clarify something you were trying to figure out? How did you get to that eureka moment?

Date:

Does your dream have anything in common with dreams you've had in the past? What themes keep reappearing in your dreams?

VISHNU, A HINDU DEITY, SLEEPING

a history of
dreaming

Long ago, humans used to sleep on and off throughout the day and night, a pattern called polyphasic sleep. (Today, we'd call that serious napping!) By 10,000 B.C., most people were sleeping through the night and getting stuff done during the day (monophasic sleep). Because they were sleeping longer—and probably having more dreams—people started to pay more attention to what played out in their minds while they slept.

Ever since, humans have remained curious about the meaning of dreams. Some people thought dreams were messages from the gods, from good or evil spirits, or even from the dead.

Others believed that dreams served as advance notice of risks, dangers, or lucky opportunities. Major religious traditions that exist today—Christianity, Judaism, Islam, and Buddhism—have passed down stories through the ages about the importance of dreams.

The word "dream" itself is centuries old. It has two origins. The Old English word "dream" meant "joy, noise, or music." In the Old Norse language, *draumr* translated as "imaginary events seen while sleeping." If you're lucky and have a good dream, both meanings are true!

> The ancient Babylonians, who lived in the area that's now the country of Iraq, generally thought that good dreams came from their gods and bad dreams came from devils.

THE ORACLE AT DELPHI

it's all Greek to me!

Ancient Greeks had a "dream team" of priests and temples to help them sort out their dreams.

Today, you might think of an incubator as something used to hatch chickens from eggs. In ancient Greece, a special kind of temple called an *asclepion* served as an incubator to hatch dreams! People would sleep there in the hopes of receiving dreams that would help them in their lives and heal their illnesses. Named for Asclepius, the Greek god of healing, these temples were home to priests who interpreted dreams and revealed the healing properties they contained.

Asclepia attracted the A-listers of Greek society. Aristocrats, politicians, soldiers, and philosophers all could be spotted there. (No paparazzi, please! No problem—cameras weren't around back then.) Visitors to an asclepion would undergo cleansing rituals—with perfumes, powders, and potions—so they'd be fresh and relaxed at bedtime and ready to have good dreams. Nighty night!

Ancient Greece's most famous dream reader was the oracle at Delphi. Considered a fortune-teller or soothsayer, the oracle at Delphi made prophesies—predictions about the future—based on dreams. Her predictions influenced powerful people's decisions about love, work, and even war.

Dreaming by the Book
Oneirocritica, a Greek book about interpreting dreams, dates back more than 1,800 years!

Get Off Me!
When you dream, chemicals in your brain paralyze your muscles. But ancient Greeks thought it happened because a demon was sitting on your chest!

HYPNOS, THE GOD OF SLEEP

All in the Family
In Greek mythology, Hypnos was the god of sleep. His twin brother, Thanatos, was the god of death. And their mother, Nyx, was the goddess of night. Word to the wise: Avoid a slumber party at THEIR house!

Date: _____

Describe your dream. Name one thing from it that surprised you. What do you think it's telling you?

_____

_____

_____

_____

_____

_____

_____

_____

_____

_____

The ancient Greek philosopher Plato **thought that** dreams came from your belly! (Maybe that explains your last stomachache ...) Today, of course, we know that dreams form in your brain.

_____

_____

_____

Date:

Have you ever had a dream about something in the future? Did it come true?

Hag Stones

In some cultures, people believed that charms or talismans could shape their dreams. In Old England, the dream tool of choice was a hag stone, a pebble with a hole in it. People believed hag stones kept away witches (also called hags) and bad dreams. If you had a bad dream, you were called hag-ridden. This is because evil female spirits—also called *maeres*—were said to sit on your chest and suffocate you. (You guessed it—that's where the word "nightmare" comes from!)

Date:

Describe your dream. What thoughts and feelings did you have when you first woke up? What thoughts and feelings do you have when you think about your dream now? If you were to choose an emoji to represent how your dream made you feel, what would it be?

Date:

Describe what happened in your dream in as few sentences as possible. Just note the basic facts: beginning, middle, and end. Now try to fill in the details. What did the dream look like? What did it sound like?

The science of studying dreams is called oneirology.

Date:

Dreams sometimes fall into one of three categories: reviewing an old event, solving a current problem, or a wish for the future. At other times, dreams defy any categories and are just plain zany!

Describe your dream. Did your dream match a category or create its own?

....

....

....

....

....

....

....

....

....

....

....

....

....

....

....

All stories have a protagonist, or main character. That's the person who performs most of the action in a story. Who was the protagonist of your last dream? Was it you? If so, what did you do? If it was someone else, did you know that person?

Date:

What was the setting in your most recent dream? Maybe it was at school, on a Broadway stage, in a major league ballpark, or (gulp!) at the dentist's office. If it was somewhere familiar, what are your associations with or memories of that place?

Date:

Was there an animal in your dream? What kind? Describe the critter's appearance and the role it played in your dream. What is your personal connection to your dream animal?

A dream animal can mean different things to different people. For example, some people associate dogs with loyalty. Others keep their distance from pooches because of fear or allergies.

Pick one image, object, or scene that really stands out in last night's dream. It might be weird, wacky, mysterious, or funny. What associations do you have with this image?

Date:

Name one thing from your dream that surprised you.
What do you think it's telling you?

Around 4,000 years ago, ancient Mesopotamians illustrated their dreams on clay tablets.

sleep takes the stage

AN ELECTROENCEPHALOGRAPH (EEG) RECORDS BRAIN WAVES.

SCIENCE OF SLEEP

Keeping an Eye on Your Dreams

One of the biggest breakthroughs on sleep and dreams came thanks to an eight-year-old boy!

In 1951, a researcher in Chicago, Illinois, U.S.A., named Eugene Aserinsky was investigating whether people's brain activity changes when they are asleep. Scientists used to think the brain slept when we slept. But Aserinsky had other ideas. He used a special machine to track and record the brain waves of his sleeping subjects.

One night, Aserinsky hooked up the machine to his eight-year-old son, Armond, to monitor his brain activity while he slept. After Armond fell asleep, his eyes started moving around like crazy under his eyelids. With each eye movement, the machine sparked to life, showing a lot of brain activity. Was Armond awake? No, he was sound asleep. Was the machine broken? No, it was working just fine.

Aserinsky had made a groundbreaking discovery: During rapid eye movement (REM) sleep, the brain isn't sleeping. It's wide awake and busy dreaming!

Scientists now know that REM sleep is one of four stages of sleep—and the stage in which most dreams happen. They're still sorting out why REM sleep happens. REM may help us refresh old memories or lock in new ones for the long term. It may help us learn new things or safely rehearse dangerous situations. Or it could be all of the above!

Even people who can't see have a REM sleep cycle. Researchers think the rapid movement of your eyes probably doesn't just point your "sight" at specific images in your dream but actually advances the scenes, like how swiping your smartphone screen with your finger brings up the next photo.

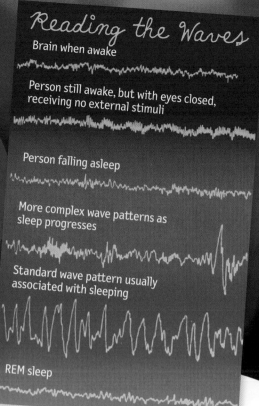

Reading the Waves

Brain when awake

Person still awake, but with eyes closed, receiving no external stimuli

Person falling asleep

More complex wave patterns as sleep progresses

Standard wave pattern usually associated with sleeping

REM sleep

The Stages of Sleep

Falling asleep at the end of the day might seem like the curtain drop at the end of a play: Show's over. Lights out. Nothing more to see here. Actually, your brain and body put on a whole different production while you sleep. Approximately every 90–120 minutes, your body cycles through four different stages of sleep.

STAGE 1
Your muscles relax. Your heart rate slows down. You drift in and out of sleep and can awaken pretty easily.

STAGE 2
Your brain waves slow down but have occasional quick bursts of activity, called spindles. You spend the longest amount of your sleeping time in stage 2.

STAGE 3
You enter deep sleep. Your brain waves become long and slow. This is the stage in which some people walk and talk in their sleep.

STAGE 4
During the REM stage, dreams happen. The body is completely still, and some muscles are frozen, but the brain is extremely active. Your heart rate and breathing slow down. When people wake up during the REM stage, they remember their dreams in far greater detail.

31

Date:

Describe what happened in your dream in as few sentences as possible. Just note the basic facts: beginning, middle, and end. Now try to fill in the details. What did the dream look like? What did it sound like?

Date:

Play the detective. Ask yourself questions about your dream.
- Whodunit?
- Where?
- Why?

DREAM
DETECTIVE

Date:

Name a connection between your dream and things that are happening in your life right now.

You were just dreaming!
- What were you dreaming about?
- What's the last image you can remember from your dream?
- Now imagine what comes next. If you had stayed asleep, what do you think would have happened? Give your dream the perfect ending!

TRY THIS!

Catch Me If I Can

Want to catch a dream in progress? Talk with your family to let them know about your experiment. Then set an alarm clock to wake yourself up in the middle of the night. Do it on the weekend, so you're not tired and grumpy for school. (And don't wake up your whole family in the process!)

Date:

Describe your dream. What thoughts and feelings did you have when you first woke up? What thoughts and feelings do you have when you think about your dream now? If you were to choose an emoji to represent how your dream made you feel, what would it be?

Date:

Did your dream last night make a lot of sense? Did it help clarify something you were trying to figure out? How did you get to that eureka moment?

Elephants stand during non-REM sleep but lie down for REM sleep.

Date:

Picture Perfect

You've heard that a picture's worth a thousand words, right? Well, let's see if pictures can capture a night's worth of dreaming!

TRY THIS!

1 Use these panels to draw your very own dream cartoon. Start by drawing only pictures—don't write any words yet. Fit in as many details as you can: clothing, scenery, facial expressions, and anything else you can remember.

2 Once you're finished drawing, add words. Don't forget to include sounds ("Boom!") and bubbles with dialogue and thoughts.

3 Share your story with your friends. Your dream might inspire the next best-selling comic-book adventure!

Date:

Dreams sometimes fall into one of three categories: reviewing an old event, solving a current problem, or a wish for the future. At other times, dreams defy any categories and are just plain zany!

Describe your dream. Did your dream match a category or create its own?

Date:

Describe what happened in your dream in as few sentences as possible. Just note the basic facts: beginning, middle, and end. Now try to fill in the details. What did the dream look like? What did it sound like?

Name one thing from your dream that surprised you. What do you think it's telling you?

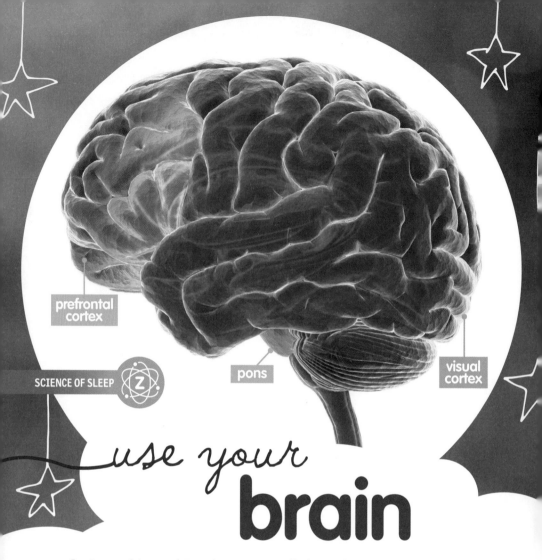

prefrontal cortex

pons

visual cortex

use your brain

Just as musicians work together to create a song, different parts of your brain team up to make a dream.

During REM sleep, your brain goes "off-line" by shutting down most of your senses. It's similar to how you would shut down a computer for a software update.

An area called the **pons** releases a chemical to temporarily paralyze some of your muscles, especially in your arms and legs. This stops you from physically acting out your dreams and possibly hurting yourself or others. This is especially important if your dreams involve, say, skydiving, mountain climbing, or fighting off a hungry lion—who happens to be your younger brother in the next bed.

The **visual cortex**—responsible for processing what we see—is more active on brain scans when we dream than when we're awake. The brain stem and limbic system—which control your feelings, desires, and memory—shift into overdrive.

The **prefrontal cortex,** the part of our brain that processes logic, shuts down. That means your brain's inner bossy pants shuts down for a bit, paving the way for your wild, weird, and illogical dreams to take the stage!

mind-blowing brain facts

There's a lot going on in your brain that you're not aware of. Noodle over these cool brain facts!

Time Out
Scientists don't know why yet, but people rarely tell time or read letters or numbers in their dreams.

Safety Check
Ever have trouble falling asleep during a sleepover at a friend's house? You're not the only one! When you sleep in unfamiliar surroundings, your brain stays half awake. Researchers think it's a safety mechanism to help us react quickly if something dangerous happens in that new setting.

SALVADOR DALÍ

Sleep Gets Surreal
There's a period of time, called the hypnagogic state, when we're not awake and not yet asleep. The famous artist Salvador Dalí—known for droopy clocks and other wild images—trained himself to be more aware during this time. He also managed to remain in that state longer in order to generate more over-the-top ideas for his artwork.

Drawing a Blank
People with a rare brain condition called Charcot-Wilbrand syndrome may not dream at all. They also can't remember images and pictures when they are awake. It's caused by an injury to the inferior lingual gyrus, part of the brain that controls our vision.

Date:

Play the detective. Ask yourself questions about your dream.
• Whodunit?
• Where?
• Why?

whodunit?

All stories have a protagonist, or main character. That's the person who performs most of the action in a story. Who was the protagonist of your last dream? Was it you? If so, what did you do? If it was someone else, did you know that person?

Date:

Your senses may be dulled to the real world when you sleep, but they're turned on in your dreams! Write down these sensory memories from your last dream:

TRY THIS!

Sight: What images and details stand out? ....
....
....

Taste: Are you eating in the dream? ....
....
....

Smell: Can you smell anything? Can you tell where in the dream the smell is coming from?
....
....

Touch: What are you holding, grabbing, or touching? ....
....
....

Making Sense(s) of Your Dreams

- Were any of your senses left out of your dream?
- Which sense was strongest?
- How did your senses move your story along?

touch?

hearing?

smell?

taste?

sight?

Hearing: Are there songs, conversations, or noises?
....

Put it all together. What is your dream telling you?
....
....
....

Date:

Does your dream have anything in common with dreams you've had in the past? What themes keep reappearing in your dreams?

Many people think that spicy foods make dreams more vivid. That's not actually true. However, a spicy taco might give you indigestion that wakes you up at night. It's during awakenings that you remember your dreams.

Date:

Describe your dream. Name one thing from
it that surprised you. What do you think it's
telling you?

Just
hanging
out.

Date:

Name a connection between your dream and things that are happening in your life right now.

Date:

Pick one image, object, or scene that really stands out from last night's dream. It might be weird, wacky, mysterious, or funny. What associations do you have with that image?

Date:

Describe what happened in your dream in as few sentences as possible. Just note the basic facts: beginning, middle, and end.
Now try to fill in the details. What did the dream look like? What did it sound like?

Date: Name a connection between your dream and things that are happening in your life right now.

TRY THIS!

Shut-Eye Solutions

It's important to get both deep and long periods of sleep in order to have a great dream night. If you're tossing and turning, try these tips to finally catch some good z's.
- Keep your room cool, dark, and quiet.
- Avoid stimulating activities, like exercise, watching TV thrillers, or texting, within an hour of bedtime.
- Try to go to bed and get up at the same time every day to put your inner clock on a predictable schedule.
- If you can't fall asleep, try one of the traditional remedies, like counting sheep, eating a bedtime snack, or reading something boring. If these don't work, develop your own shortcut to dreamland!

Play the detective. Ask yourself questions about your dream.
• Whodunit?
• Where?
• Why?

A team of researchers in Chicago discovered that zebra finches seem to "practice" their songs in their dreams. How can they tell? The exact same parts of the bird's brain are active when dreaming and when singing!

nice catch

You're not the only one who hates it when you have a nightmare. Long ago, mothers in the Ojibwe tribe, from around the Great Lakes, came up with a creative solution to protect their children from scary dreams: a dream catcher.

They wove string around a circular or oval frame made of willow branch to make it look like a spiderweb, with a hole left open in the middle. Then they hung feathers beneath it. They believed nightmares would get caught in the net and dry up in the sun's rays in the daytime. They thought happy dreams would either pass through the hole in the middle or travel down the feathers, into the mind of the sleeping child.

The dream catchers were not made to last. The materials would break down as the child got older and was better able to process and learn from scary dreams.

Other Native American tribes adopted the dream catcher tradition, too. And since then, dream catchers have become popular around the world.

Make Your Own Dream Catcher

What You'll Need:
- A paper plate
- A ruler
- A pencil
- Scissors
- A hole punch
- 6 feet (2 m) of yarn (pick a favorite color)
- 9 small plastic or glass colored beads
- 3 plastic craft feathers
- Colored markers or crayons

Optional:
- Paint, stickers, glitter, glue, or anything else to decorate your dream catcher!

If you'd like to paint the plate beforehand, let it dry completely before starting these next steps.

STEPS:

1. Measure two inches (5 cm) into the plate from the edge and make a dot. Do this in several spots around the edge of the plate.

2. Connect your dots to form a circle.

3. Cut along the circle line to create a big hole in the paper plate.

4. Punch 9 or 10 equally spaced holes, close to the inside edge of the plate rim, leaving enough space so that the holes don't rip through the edge.

5. Thread the yarn through one hole. Tie a big knot at the end that's at the back of the plate.

6. Weave the yarn through each hole, along the edges of the plate, in a circle. Make sure the yarn isn't too tight.
   Once the yarn has gone through each hole, thread it through the yarn loops you created between the holes, in a circular pattern. This should pull the yarn toward the center of the big hole. Keep threading the yarn in this way until you have a pattern you like.

7. When you finish your pattern, pull the yarn gently and tie it in a knot around a hole or another part of the yarn. Decorate the plate however you want.

8. Punch three holes close together at the bottom of the plate, near the outer edge, being careful not to punch through any yarn.

9. Cut three six- to eight-inch (15 to 20 cm) pieces of yarn.

10. Slip three beads onto each piece of yarn. Then tie a feather to the bottom of each piece.

11. Tie the top of one of the short pieces of yarn to one of the three holes at the bottom of the plate. Repeat with the other two pieces of yarn.

12. Punch a last hole at the top of the plate, near the outer edge, being careful not to punch through any yarn.

13. Through that top hole, thread a piece of yarn to the length you like and tie a knot so you can hang your dream catcher above your bed.

Sweet dreams!

Date:

Name a connection between your dream and things that are happening in your life right now.

....

....

....

....

....

....

....

....

....

....

....

....

....

....

....

....

Dreams sometimes fall into one of three categories: reviewing an old event, solving a current problem, or a wish for the future. At other times, dreams defy any categories and are just plain zany!
    Describe your dream. Did your dream match a category or create its own?

Date:

Name one thing from your dream that surprised you.
What do you think it's telling you?

Date:

Dreaming on Repeat

Reruns aren't just for TV shows. Some dreams repeat themselves, too! Recurring dreams may teach you new things about old events. Or they might help you process something more fully, so you can then "delete" it from your mental file.

TRY THIS!

If your latest dream is a "been there, done that" dream, ask yourself:

When did you first have the dream?

What details have changed?

Why might this dream have returned right now?

What issues, challenges, or changes are you facing in real life?

Date:

All stories have a protagonist, or main character. That's the person who performs most of the action in a story. Who was the protagonist of your last dream? Was it you? If so, what did you do? If it was someone else, did you know that person?

....

....

....

....

....

....

....

....

....

....

....

....

....

....

Date:

Was there an animal in your dream? What kind? Describe the critter's appearance and the role it played in your dream. What is your personal connection to your dream animal?

Big cats pull down some major z's. Lions sleep 5–10 hours a day, and tigers sleep up to 20 hours!

Date:

What was the setting in your most recent dream? If it was somewhere familiar, what are your associations with or memories of that place?

Think about last night's dream. What did you like about it, if anything? If you could change anything about it, what would you change?

TEMPLE OF SERAPIS
IN LUXOR, EGYPT

HISTORY & CULTURE

Dream Like an Egyptian

Ancient Egyptian pharaohs believed the gods sent important messages, called *omina*, through dreams. (Think of them as ZZZ-mail.) The omina (or omens) weren't always clear. So the pharaohs would visit temples dedicated to Serapis, the god of dreams. There they would consult with priests called "the masters of secret things." The priests would help interpret dreams and not gossip about the details.

Date:

Play the detective. Ask yourself questions about your dream.
- Whodunit?
- Where?
- Why?

Name a connection between your dream and things that are happening in your life right now.

scary stuff

You've heard the phrase "What a nightmare!" Maybe you've had a nightmare or two (or several) yourself. Well, what exactly ARE nightmares? These scary dreams are tied to a part of the brain called the **amygdala** (ah-MIG-da-la). It's in charge of the intense, negative emotions you feel, such as anger or fear. The amygdala is super active during the REM stage of sleep. But another part of your brain called the **prefrontal cortex**—the part that normally filters out or helps control intense feelings—is asleep at that time. That means fear and other strong emotions can more easily slip into the story line of your dreams.

These story lines change as you grow up. Toddlers often have nightmares about getting lost from their parents. Preschool kids have scary dreams about the dark or monsters. Older kids have nightmares about real-life situations, like being late for an exam.

Nightmares aren't fun, but they're perfectly normal. Researchers think they might help you prepare for difficult situations or identify a challenge or fear that you may need to face in the light of day.

Only about 20 to 40 percent of children ages 5 to 12 have frequent nightmares. However, these bad dreams can be triggered by watching scary movies, reading horror stories, or even telling spooky stories to your friends at a sleepover right before bedtime. So you might want to switch to something silly or happy before you turn off the lights!

stressing out *in* *your sleep*

You're late to class. There's a test you didn't know about. You look down and—gasp!—you're not wearing any clothes! These dreams—called anxiety dreams—can start in your tween years and pop up throughout your lifetime. We all have them. Here are some questions to ask yourself the next time you find yourself squirming in your sleep with one of these common anxiety dreams.

1. You're unprepared for a test.

Are you being too hard on yourself? Have you set too many goals at once?

2. You're late for class.

Are you stressed out by deadlines?

How can you set your goals but still set aside time for fun?

3. You lose control of your bike, or you're in a car that loses control.

Do you feel out of control of a certain situation? Do you want to put the brakes on something in your life?

4. You can't find a bathroom.

In this case, you probably have a full bladder and your body is giving you physical cues that get written into your dream. (Imagine your character suddenly saying, "Be right back—I need a bathroom break!") But it might also suggest that you feel embarrassed about something.

What questions can you come up with for these other common anxiety dreams?

1. You're naked in public. ....

....

2. You're flying. (This one can also be fun, too, not scary.) ....

....

3. You're falling from a cliff. ....

....

4. You find an unfamiliar room in a place you know. ....

....

Date: _____

Work Through Your Nightmare

TRY THIS!

The next time you get spooked in your sleep by a bad dream, try these tips to shed some light—and humor—on the scary situation. Write down the scary dream in detail. Take your time. Writing it down helps get it out of your head.

1 Describe the dream to someone close to you. Ask what they think. Saying it out loud to someone you trust helps make sense of the nightmare.

2 Think about how you could take control in the bad dream. Imagine yourself triumphing over evil or escaping from a scary maze. Have fun: the stranger the solution, the better! (For example, give a funny name to scary characters. After all, how terrifying can an alien named Petunia really be?)

3 How could you change the plot or characters? For example, transform that creepy ocean creature into a harmless goldfish! When you take a scary image and change it so it becomes harmless, psychologists call that image rehearsal. They recommend practicing it a few times each day, in order to lock in those positive and playful replacements. That helps rewrite the script for your bad dream so it has a new, happy ending!

Date:

Name one thing from your dream that surprised you.
What do you think it's telling you?

_____

_____

_____

_____

_____

_____

_____

_____

_____

_____

_____

_____

_____

_____

_____

_____

Date:

Pick one image, object, or scene that really stands out in last night's dream. It might be weird, wacky, mysterious, or funny. What associations do you have with that image?

Date:

Name a connection between your dream and things that are happening in your life right now.

....

....

....

....

....

....

....

....

....

....

....

Think about last night's dream. What did you like about it, if anything? If you could change anything about it, what would you change?

In Hawaiian mythology, dreams are referred to as "soul sleep." The soul was thought to leave and re-enter the body through a person's tear ducts.

Date:

Describe what happened in your dream in as few sentences as possible. Just note the basic facts: beginning, middle, and end. Now try to fill in the details. What did the dream look like? What did it sound like?

You've probably heard of jet lag. How about dream lag? That's what happens when there is a five-to-seven-day delay between when an event happens in real life and when it appears in your dreams.

Date:

Play the detective. Ask yourself questions about your dream.
• Whodunit?
• Where?
• Why?

Date: _____

Describe your dream. Does it have anything in common with dreams you've had in the past? What themes keep reappearing in your dreams?

....

....

....

Dreams at the start of the night tend to feature recent events. Dreams later in the night often involve situations from your past.

....

....

....

....

....

....

....

....

....

....

....

Date:

Dreams sometimes fall into one of three categories: reviewing an old event, solving a current problem, or a wish for the future. At other times, dreams defy any categories and are just plain zany!

Describe your dream. Did your dream match a category or create its own?

why do we dream, really?

Experts have several ideas about the meaning of dreams and the role that dreams play in your life. But just like you and your siblings, these experts don't always agree.

Some scientists think of dreams as a sideshow to the main act your brain performs: keeping you alive and alert when you're awake. Even at night when you're fast asleep, the brain controls your breathing and heartbeat. It takes in information from your five senses so that you can react to loud noises (Pow!). It removes unnecessary or repetitive information (like every step you took during the day), just like when you clear out your computer's hard drive. It trims some connections between cells in the brain and helps maintain others to help you learn. As your brain cranks through these many tasks, scientists think it churns out dreams as a by-product—kind of like a mental burp.

Some psychologists think that dreams were a nighttime "dress rehearsal" that helped our ancient ancestors through dangerous situations they encountered in the act of daily survival. For example, a dream about a snake might have made our ancestors more aware of any snakes that crossed their path during the day. (That's *sssome sssmart* dreaming!)

Other psychotherapists and counselors see dreams differently. They think dreams contain important symbols and themes that can help you solve personal problems and lead a more meaningful life. Your dreams might tell you about feelings you've been avoiding or something you really hope will happen.

For these specialists, dreams are like a highly personalized puzzle that only you can piece together. Unlike a puzzle showing cute kittens or pretty scenery, though, your dream puzzle might sometimes spell out WARNING! WARNING! Dreams can serve as an early warning system, like a thunderstorm alert on your phone, to lead you to make important changes in your life. For example, if a frenemy pops up in your dreams, it may be because you're confused by that person's behavior and it's time to work things out.

Which of these dream theories is the right one? We really don't know, but they all offer something to noodle over with your wonderful, mysterious brain.

Date:

Was there an animal in your dream? What kind? Describe the critter's appearance and the role it played in your dream. What is your personal connection to your dream animal?

Birds **have periods of** REM sleep **that** last about five seconds. **They even take** in-flight naps **on** long journeys.

Date:

Name a connection between your dream and things that are happening in your life right now.

Date:

Pick one image, object, or scene that really stands out in last night's dream. It might be weird, wacky, mysterious, or funny. Let yourself play with options. What associations do you have with that image?

Date:

Describe your dream. What thoughts and feelings did you have when you first woke up? What thoughts and feelings do you have when you think about your dream now? If you were to choose an emoji to represent how your dream made you feel, what would it be?

Date:

Describe what happened in your dream in as few sentences as possible. Just note the basic facts: beginning, middle, and end. Now try to fill in the details. What did the dream look like? What did it sound like?

The Perfect Solution

What is the number one problem or challenge stumping you these days? In what areas do you feel stuck? Some experts believe that you use your dreams to help uncover part of the solution.

Tell yourself several nights in a row that you're going to dream up an answer, and see what plays out. Don't sweat it if it takes time for this to work. Even if nothing comes directly from your dreams, you're still making a real effort to reflect on your problem. And don't make any big changes based on a dream until you've talked about your discoveries with a person you trust.

TRY THIS!

When you wake up, ask yourself:

What feelings did you experience in your dream? How might they relate to your problem?

....

....

....

Any surprises? New information? Clues about what's wrong? ....

....

....

....

Did the story line of your dream include any real steps you can take next? ....

....

....

....

Date:

Play the detective. Ask yourself questions about your dream.
- Whodunit?
- Where?
- Why?

TOP SECRET

Some people dream in black and white!

Date:

Describe your dream. Name one thing from it that surprised you.
What do you think it's telling you?

HISTORY & CULTURE

Maya Worry Dolls

In the Maya culture, some people believe
that "worry dolls," or "trouble dolls," help them
have a good night's sleep. They can tell their
concerns to this small doll—made of yarn and
wood—and then tuck the doll under their
pillow. The doll does all the worrying for you
while you sleep, so you can wake up refreshed
and trouble free.

87

Date:

Describe your dream. Does it have anything in common with dreams you've had in the past? What themes keep reappearing in your dreams?

Date:

All stories have a protagonist, or main character. That's the person who performs most of the action in a story. Who was the protagonist of your last dream? Was it you? If so, what did you do? If it was someone else, did you know that person?

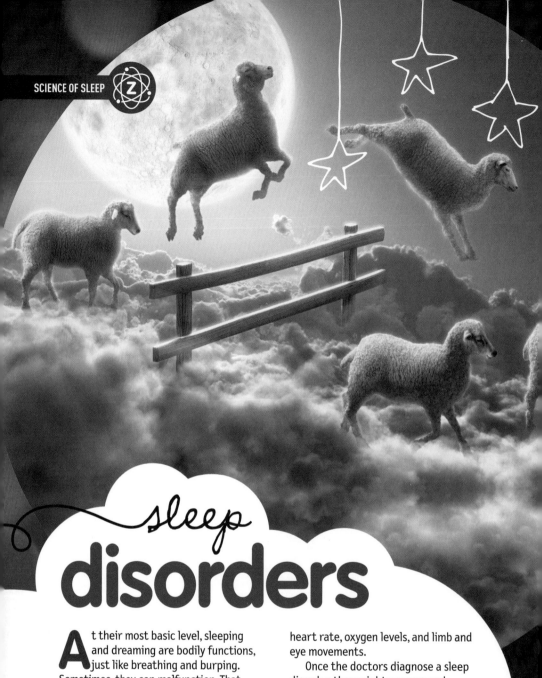

sleep disorders

At their most basic level, sleeping and dreaming are bodily functions, just like breathing and burping. Sometimes, they can malfunction. That "glitch" is called a sleep disorder. That's when sleep science can help!

To diagnose a sleep disorder, patients head to a sleep lab, a place where doctors can observe and monitor people while they sleep. They use cameras and sensors to measure a patient's brain waves, breathing, heart rate, oxygen levels, and limb and eye movements.

Once the doctors diagnose a sleep disorder, they might recommend different solutions. Some people might need to take a medication. Others may need to change their diet or lifestyle. Still others may need to use breathing equipment at night. All are important prescriptions that can help a patient heal and get a good night's sleep!

With some sleep disorders, people sometimes do unexplainable or even dangerous things in their sleep. Fortunately, sleep specialists can help people overcome these disorders and keep themselves safe. Here are some of the most common sleep disorders:

Narcolepsy

is a condition in which people suddenly fall asleep at any time, even during the daytime. It's caused when the brain zooms directly into REM sleep, without gradually passing through the first stages of sleep. This can be dangerous because people can fall down and injure themselves.

Night terrors

happen mostly to children ages three to six. They're not nightmares because there's no dreaming involved. Instead, the nervous system releases an intense charge while the person sleeps. Breathing and heartbeat speed up, so that the person feels both wired and terrified. They might scream and cry in their sleep. Fortunately, they almost never remember the episode afterward and go back to sleep.

Parasomnias

are sleep disorders that happen during the non-REM stage of sleep. A person gets up—without waking up—and performs activities that they don't remember afterward. Sleepwalking is probably the most well-known one. It happens the most among kids ages five to 12. People also sleep talk (called somniloquy) and even sleep laugh! (Must have been a good joke ...) Even more worrisome, some people do such elaborate things as cooking a meal in their sleep or getting in a car and trying to drive.

Date:

Was there an animal in your dream? What kind? Describe the critter's appearance and the role it played in your dream. What is your personal connection to your dream animal?

....

....

....

....

....

....

....

....

....

....

....

....

....

....

....

....

Date:

What was the setting in your most recent dream? If it was somewhere familiar, what are your associations with or memories of that place?

Date:

Name a connection between your dream and things that are happening in your life right now.

....

....

....

....

....

....

....

....

....

....

....

Sleepy Puppies

Two drowsy dogs helped scientists make a big leap in sleep and brain research. In 1973, scientists at Stanford University in California, U.S.A., studied two Doberman pinschers that kept falling down, fast asleep. They had narcolepsy! The researchers identified the specific genetic mutation—change in the dogs' DNA—that affected the dogs' brain chemistry. That single glitch is what caused the narcolepsy that made the pooches pass out.

Dreams sometimes fall into one of three categories: reviewing an old event, solving a current problem, or a wish for the future. At other times, dreams defy any categories and are just plain zany!

Describe your dream. Did your dream match a category or create its own?

Dogs dream, too! They sometimes twitch, growl, whimper, wiggle, and wag their tails as they're dreaming.

Date:

Banish Your Bad Dreams

Drain a nightmare of its scare power with these simple suggestions. Use the space on these pages to sketch your ideas.

TRY THIS!

1
Draw pictures of the disturbing characters in your dream—but make them funny! You might try putting them in a ridiculous costume or giving them an extra-large clown nose.

2

Turn yourself
into a dream-busting
superhero. Sketch your
fabulous costume and
your special powers (like
laser fingers—
Zap! Zap!).

Date: _____

Was there anything funny about your dream? What was it?
What made it funny?

....
....
....
....
....
....
....
....
....
....
....
....
....
....
....

Date:

Does your dream have anything in common with dreams you've had in the past? What themes keep reappearing in your dreams?

Want a good night's sleep? Wear socks to bed. They help regulate your body temperature, a key to deep sleep.

Date:

Name one thing from your dream that surprised you. What do you think it's telling you?

Pick one image, object, or scene that really stands out in last night's dream. It might be weird, wacky, mysterious, or funny. Let yourself play with options. What associations do you have with that image?

interpreting dreams
by the book

When you come across a word you don't know or understand, you look it up in a dictionary. Where can you turn if a dream has you baffled? A dream dictionary! These popular reference books describe common elements in dreams, including themes, categories, words, and images.

A dream dictionary interprets these dream elements using mythology, fairy tales, and psychology. Because they interpret each item to have the same meaning in *every* dream, dream dictionaries suggest that some dreams have a universal meaning across time and cultures. For example, a dog always symbolizes loyalty. A snake represents betrayal.

But ... what if you love snakes but hate dogs? Your interpretation might be different than the dictionary's version, based on your personal experiences. That's OK! It's more important to understand your own unique interpretation of your dreams. Just think of the dream dictionary as a fun, interesting read that can offer a new way to look at familiar things. You might not look at a dog in the same way ever again!

Look It Up!

Can a dictionary help you figure out dreams?

Give a dream dictionary a try! Start by writing down an important element in your most recent dream. It could be a person, place, animal, or thing (for example, a bee).

Next, write down all your personal associations—past and present—with this word ("I was stung by a bee once" or "I love honey").

Think about what might have triggered this element to appear in your dream. Did it come up in conversation? Did you read about it or see it online? (Maybe you heard the phrase "a busy bee.")

Have you dreamed about this element before? When? What's different this time?

Now look up the element in a dream dictionary. Read through the description and see how your dream compares with the book's interpretation.

What Does It All Mean?

Check out these dream dictionary interpretations of familiar items. What do you think? Would you interpret them the same way?

Rainbow: Good luck

Broom: Sweeping away problems

Throne: Power

Tarantula: Fear

Eagle: Fame, power

Date:

Dreaming the Rainbow

Certain colors may remind you of your favorite people or events in life. Maybe your best friend always wears blue, or your favorite stuffed animal is a pink teddy bear. Explore the spectrum of colors and symbols that pop up in your dream!

TRY THIS!

List all the colors in your dream. What do you associate with each color?

Many people associate certain colors with different feelings. Do you agree with these common color interpretations?

Blue = Sad

Green = Jealous

Yellow = Happy

Red = Angry

What was the setting in your most recent dream?
If it was somewhere familiar, what are your associations
with or memories of that place?

Date:

Describe your dream. Name a connection between your dream and things that are happening in your life right now.

....

....

....

....

....

....

....

....

....

The Doctor Is In
Insights From Psychiatry

Every field has its superstars. When it comes to the scientific study of the brain and human behavior—including dreaming!—the A-listers are two psychiatrists named Sigmund Freud and Carl Jung.

In 1899, Freud wrote the book *The Interpretation of Dreams.* He thought dreams could reveal secrets and embarrassing feelings and situations from our past that we don't like to think about.

SIGMUND FREUD

CARL JUNG

Carl Jung—a frenemy of Freud's—thought dreams are messages about living a happier here and now. He found that dreams have archetypes, or common images and themes that are the same for people all over the world.

A lot has changed since Freud and Jung came up with their groundbreaking ideas. But many psychotherapists and counselors today still use their insights to help patients work through emotions, wishes, and events in their lives.

Date:

Describe what happened in your dream in as few sentences as possible. Just note the basic facts: beginning, middle, and end.

Now try to fill in the details. What did the dream look like? What did it sound like?

DREAM

Date:

Play the detective. Ask yourself questions about your dream.
- Whodunit?
- Where?
- Why?

Was there anything funny about your dream? What was it? What made it funny?

Some scientists think that 30,000-year-old cave paintings in France are pictures of dreams!

Date:

Describe your dream. Does it have anything in common with dreams you've had in the past? What themes keep reappearing in your dreams?

Did your dream last night make a lot of sense? Did it help clarify something you were trying to figure out? How did you get to that eureka moment?

Date: _____

Was there an animal in your dream? What kind? Describe the critter's appearance and the role it played in your dream. What is your personal connection to your dream animal?

....

....

....

....

....

....

....

....

....

....

....

....

....

....

Date:

Describe your dream. What thoughts and feelings did you have when you first woke up? What thoughts and feelings do you have when you think about it now? If you were to choose an emoji to represent how your dream made you feel, what would it be?

lucid dreams:
Lights! Camera! Action!

Have you ever been in the middle of a dream and realized, *Hey, this isn't real. I'm dreaming!* That's called lucid dreaming. It's pretty cool, because during lucid dreams you can sometimes use your willpower to change and direct what's happening in the dream itself.

Lucid dreams are most common among children up to around age 16, but some adults have them, too. Athletes sometimes rehearse sports moves in their lucid dreams. Other people use lucid dreams to help deal with anxieties, low self-esteem, or recurring nightmares because they can build in positive messages and story lines.

Admittedly, some experts aren't convinced that lucid dreaming is helpful. But it can still be a lot of fun! So are you ready to sit in the director's chair and give lucid dreaming a try? Getting a good night's sleep should be your top priority, so check with an adult before trying these exercises.

1. Ask yourself throughout the day: "Am I awake? Am I alert?" Repeat this often enough, and you might be able to ask yourself the same question in your dream.
2. Look at your face in a mirror several times a day. Having a clear sense of how you look will enable you to notice in dreams when your appearance changes. That's a big clue that you're asleep and dreaming!
3. Tell yourself, "Tonight, I'm going lucid!"
4. Once you realize you're in a dream, add in whatever plot or details you like! (For example: free ice cream for everyone!)

TRY THIS!

become a
dream whiz

There's more than one way to wrangle your dreams. Try these other techniques!

Incubate a Dream Like the Ancient Greeks

1. Write down a question about your life you want answered before you go to bed.
2. Say it out loud to help it sink into your unconscious mind.
3. In bed, close your eyes and visualize the question like a movie in your mind. Go scene by scene, frame by frame.
4. Tell yourself you really want an answer during that night of sleep.
5. Don't jump right out of bed in the morning. Think about the question and see what answers come up.
6. Keep your dream journal handy throughout the day. More solutions may pop up as you go through your day!

Become a Dream Reporter

Journalists know how to tell a story so that they cover all of its most important details. To do that, they ask themselves the five W's and one H: who, what, where, why, when, and how. Now try it for yourself!

WHO was in your dream?

WHAT was the story line of your dream?

WHERE did the dream happen?

WHY were certain details there?

WHEN did the action take place (past/present/future)?

HOW did you feel during and after the dream?

115

Date:

Describe what happened in your dream in as few sentences as possible. Just note the basic facts: beginning, middle, and end. Now try to fill in the details. What did the dream look like? What did it sound like?

The average person has around four dreams per night. That equals 1,460 dreams each year—and some 100,000 dreams in a lifetime!

Date:

Name a connection between your dream and things that are happening in your life right now.

Date:

Play the detective. Ask yourself questions about your dream.
- Whodunit?
- Where?
- Why?

All stories have a protagonist, or main character. That's the person who performs most of the action in a story. Who was the protagonist of your last dream? Was it you? If so, what did you do? If it was someone else, did you know that person?

Date:

What was the setting in your most recent dream? If it was somewhere familiar, what are your associations with or memories of that place?

Pick one image, object, or scene that really stands out in last night's dream. It might be weird, wacky, mysterious, or funny. What associations do you have with that image?

Date:

Bedtime Stories

All books and movies have story lines. Your dreams usually do, too—even if they're super strange. The story is what people tend to remember most about their dreams. Use these tips to recall the story that unfolded in your dream.

TRY THIS!

1 Write down your dream as a story, with a beginning, middle, and end. Include dialogue: What did you and your characters say?

2 Pay attention to specific words or phrases in your dream; they might be important clues. (For example: Why does Mom have blue hair? And why does she keep saying, "Where's my dinosaur?")

3

Start with a rough draft and then fill in more details as you remember them.

Date:

Dreams sometimes fall into one of three categories: reviewing an old event, solving a current problem, or a wish for the future. At other times, dreams defy any categories and are just plain zany!
Describe your dream. Did your dream match a category or create its own?

....
....
....
....
....
....
....
....
....
....
....
....
....
....
....

Name one thing from your dream that surprised you. What do you think it's telling you?

The *Tetris* effect (named after the block-building video game) is when a person's daytime obsessions show up in their dreams.

can dreams make me rich and famous?

W e all dream, but some people are *dreamers*. They follow their imaginations—both while awake and asleep—to amazing new places and ideas. These people all found incredible inspiration in their dreams that led to fame, fortune, and success!

FRANKENSTEIN

Read All About It

Frankenstein's monster has a starring role in horror movies and nightmares. No wonder, then, that the plot and main characters of the novel *Frankenstein* came to author Mary Shelley in her dreams! Fellow author Robert Louis Stevenson also lured a creepy character out of his dreams and onto the page. He dreamed up the starring character of his famous novel, *The Strange Case of Dr. Jekyll and Mr. Hyde.*

MR. HYDE

Seems Sew Right

Elias Howe was building his new invention, the sewing machine, but he was stuck. What kind of needle should he use? One night, he dreamed he was attacked by warriors whose spears had holes in the tips. Eureka! Sewing machines to this day use needles with holes in the tips.

Sleepy Songwriting

The Beatles are one of the best-selling bands in history, in part because they found inspiration where other musicians didn't. Band member Paul McCartney woke up one morning with a melody in his head. He headed to the piano and played the tune from his dreams. That song—"Yesterday"—reached number one on the charts!

Sssuper Idea

For German scientist August Kekulé, a dream snake equaled a brilliant idea! He dreamed of a snake eating its own tail. He used that image to design a model of how atoms fit together in the molecule of the chemical benzene.

Google This!

Where would you find information if you didn't have Google? Computer scientist Larry Page found an important idea in his dreams. One day he woke up from a dream asking himself, "What if we could download the whole web and just keep the links?" That inspiration led to the launch of the Google search engine!

Fore!

Champion golfer Jack Nicklaus was on a losing streak. He just couldn't seem to hit the ball right. One night, he noticed that he held his golf club differently in his dream than he did in reality. He tried out the new grip on the golf course—and started winning again!

127

Date:

All stories have a protagonist, or main character. That's the person who performs most of the action in a story. Who was the protagonist of your last dream? Was it you? If so, what did you do? If it was someone else, did you know that person?

Date:

Does your dream have anything in common with dreams you've had in the past? What themes keep reappearing in your dreams?

Date: _____

Name one thing from your dream that surprised you.
What do you think it's telling you?

_____

_____

_____

_____

_____

_____

_____

_____

_____

_____

_____

_____

_____

_____

In the African country of Liberia, the Dan people create masks to represent spirits that have visited them in their dreams. They then wear the masks to perform dances and skits at village festivals.

Date:

Pick one image, object, or scene that really stands out in last night's dream. It might be weird, wacky, mysterious, or funny. What associations do you have with that image?

Date:

Name a connection between your dream and things that are happening in your life right now.

Dream Vacation

In ancient China, it was believed that while a person dreamed, their soul left their body for the dream world. It was not a good idea to wake up a sleeping person because their spirit might not ever find its way back to the body.

Date:

Describe your dream. What thoughts and feelings did you have when you first woke up? What thoughts and feelings do you have when you think about your dream now? If you were to choose an emoji to represent how your dream made you feel, what would it be?

Date:

Describe what happened in your dream in as few sentences as possible. Just note the basic facts: beginning, middle, and end.
Now try to fill in the details. What did the dream look like? What did it sound like?

Date:

Play the detective. Ask yourself questions about your dream.
- Whodunit?
- Where?
- Why?

Date:

Was there an animal in your dream? What kind? Describe the critter's appearance and the role it played in your dream. What is your personal connection to your dream animal?

....

....

....

....

....

....

....

....

....

....

....

....

....

....

....

....

Date:

What was the setting in your most recent dream? If it was somewhere familiar, what are your associations with or memories of that place?

Amphibians and fish don't have REM cycles when they sleep.

Date:

Did your dream last night make a lot of sense? Did it help clarify something you were trying to figure out? How did you get to that eureka moment?

Date:

Give Me Five!

TRY THIS!

1
Pick your top five favorite dreams.

2
Write down what makes each of them stand out. What has changed over time?

3
Feel free to swap dream stories with your friends!

dream big

By now, you've tried a lot of different exercises and ways of figuring out your dreams.

Which ones have worked best? Which ones are your favorites?

In this journal, we've talked about the dreams that happen when you're asleep.

But dreaming also happens when you're awake. When you're encouraged to dream big, it means to set your goals high and reach for the stars.

As First Lady Eleanor Roosevelt once said, "The future belongs to those who believe in the beauty of their dreams."

Nighttime dreams can help fuel lifetime dreams. They can reveal to us what really matters, what we want to change, and our wishes for the future.

So dream big—night and day.

dream
manifesto

A Dream Manifesto for Lifelong Learning From Your Dreams

We all dream.

Dreaming is a mysterious gift from our brains.

You can remember your dreams if you work at it.

That work is part play, part science, and part imagination.

Understanding dreams is a lifelong process.

Pay attention. The meanings of your dreams can change.

Keep a dream journal. Compare your dreams over time.

Never judge a dream. Sometimes it might provide important clues about your true self—and sometimes it might be just a fun, silly stroll through fantasyland.

Stay open, curious, and flexible.

Trying to understand your dreams can become an important part of understanding yourself, your relationships, and your world, both inside and out.

Dreams can change the world. They already have!

Dream on!

index

Boldface indicates
illustrations.

A
Age of dreamer
  amount of sleep needed 12
  characters in dreams 7
  lucid dreams 114
  night terrors 91
  nightmares 66
  remembering dreams 14
  sleep disorders 91
  sleepwalking 91
Amphibians, sleep in 137
Amygdala 66
Ancient cultures 18–21, **18–21**
  Babylon 18
  China 132
  Egypt 63, **63**
  Greece 19, **19**, 20, **20**, 115, **115**
  hag stones 21, **21**
  Hindu **18**
  Mesopotamia 29, **29**
Animals
  dreaming 53
  journal entries 7, 27, 61, 80, 92, 102,
    103, 112, 136
  sleep 61, **61**, 80, 137
Anxiety dreams 67
Asclepia (Greek temples) 19
Aserinsky, Armond 30
Aserinsky, Eugene 30

B
Babylonians 18
Bad dreams
  anxiety dreams 67
  nightmares 7, 21, 54–55, **54–55**, 66,
    68, 96–97
Bathrooms, dreams about 67
Beatles (band) 127, **127**
Benzene 127, **127**
Big cats 61, **61**
Birds
  dreaming 53
  in dreams 103
  sleep 80
Brain
  amygdala 66
  electroencephalograph (EEG) **30**
  facts 43
  number of connections 4
  parts 42, **42**
  scans 72, **72**
  during sleep 30, 31, **31**, 78
  waves 31, **31**
  weight 4
Brooms, in dreams 103

C
Cartooning 38
Cave paintings 109, **109**
Charcot-Wilbrand syndrome 43
Children see Age of dreamer
China, ancient 132
Colors in dreams 86, 104

D
Dalí, Salvador 43, **43**
Dan people 130, **130**

Delphi oracle 19, **19**
Dogs
  dreaming 95
  in dreams 27, **27**, 102
  sleep research 94, **94**
Dream big 140
Dream catchers 54–55, **54–55**
Dream dictionaries 102–103
Dream journaling
  animal dreams 27, 61, 80, 92, 112,
    136
  basic facts and details 11, 23, 32,
    40, 51, 74, 84, 107, 116, 134
  cartooning 38
  categories of dreams 24, 39, 57, 77,
    95, 124
  clarifying things 16, 37, 111, 138
  colors 104
  common themes 17, 47, 76, 88, 99,
    110, 129
  connection to real life 14, 34, 49,
    52, 56, 65, 72, 81, 94, 106, 117, 132
  detective questions 33, 44, 53, 64,
    75, 86, 108, 118, 135
  favorite dreams 139
  funny things 98, 109
  future, dreams about 21
  nightmares 68, 96–97
  perfect endings 35
  problem-solving 85
  protagonist 25, 45, 60, 89, 119, 128
  recurring dreams 59
  scary dreams 68
  sensory memories 46
  setting 13, 26, 62, 93, 105, 120, 137
  stand-out images 22, 28, 50, 71, 82,
    101, 121, 131
  story lines 122–123
  surprises 20, 29, 41, 48, 58, 70, 87,
    100, 125, 130
  thoughts and feelings 10, 23, 36, 83,
    113, 133
  what you like or would change 12,
    63, 73
  word association tree 15
Dream lag 74
Dream manifesto 141
Dreams
  catching in progress 35
  as inspiration 126–127, **126–127**
  interpreting 102–103
  length of 8
  number per night 116
  past events in 76
  problem-solving 85
  purpose of 78–79
  recent events in 76
  remembering 8–9, 14
  scientific predictions about 72
  Tetris effect 125, **125**
  time of night and 76
  types of dreams 7

E
Eagles, in dreams 103
Egypt, ancient 63, **63**
Electroencephalograph (EEG) **30**
Elephants 37, **37**
England, hag stones 21, **21**

F
Falling, dreams about 67
Fantastic dreams 7
Favorite dreams 139
Fish, sleep in 137
Flying, dreams about 67
Frankenstein (Shelley) 126, **126**
Freud, Sigmund 106, **106**
Future, dreams about 21

G
Google search engine 127, **127**
Greece, ancient 19, **19**, 20, **20**, 115, **115**

H
Hag stones 21, **21**
Hawaiian mythology 73
History of dreaming 18–21, **18–21**
Howe, Elias 126
Hypnos (god of sleep) **19**

I
Insomnia, avoiding 52
Interpreting dreams 102–103

J
Journaling see Dream journaling
Journalism questions 115
Jung, Carl 106, **106**

K
Kekulé, August 127
Kids see Age of dreamer

L
Laughing in your sleep 91
Liberia, mask 130, **130**
Lions 61
Lucid dreaming 114–115

M
Masks 130, **130**
Maya worry dolls 87, **87**
McCartney, Paul 127
Memory
  remembering dreams 8–9
  sleep as aid to 81
Mesopotamians 29, **29**
Monophasic sleep 18

N
Nakedness, dreams about 67
Napping 18
Narcolepsy 91, 94
Native American traditions 54, **54**
Nicklaus, Jack 127, **127**
Night terrors 91
Nightmares
  brain and 66
  defined 7
  dream catchers as protection
    from 54–55, **54–55**
  dream journaling 96–97
  frequency 66
  word origin 21
  working through 68, 96–97
Nyx (goddess of night) 19

credits

Dr. ALLAN PETERKIN is a professor of psychiatry and family medicine at the University of Toronto, where he heads the program in Health, Arts, and Humanities. He is the author of 14 books for adults and children. He is especially interested in what makes humans curious, creative, and healthy.

Text Copyright © 2019 Allan Peterkin
Compilation Copyright © 2019 National Geographic Partners, LLC

Since 1888, the National Geographic Society has funded more than 12,000 research, exploration, and preservation projects around the world. The Society receives funds from National Geographic Partners, LLC, funded in part by your purchase. A portion of the proceeds from this book supports this vital work. To learn more, visit natgeo.com/info.

NATIONAL GEOGRAPHIC and Yellow Border Design are trademarks of the National Geographic Society, used under license.

For more information, visit nationalgeographic.com, call 1-800-647-5463, or write to the following address:

National Geographic Partners
1145 17th Street N.W.
Washington, D.C. 20036-4688 U.S.A.

Visit us online at nationalgeographic .com/books

For librarians and teachers: ngchildrensbooks.org

More for kids from National Geographic: natgeokids.com

National Geographic Kids magazine inspires children to explore their world with fun yet educational articles on animals, science, nature, and more. Using fresh storytelling and amazing photography, *Nat Geo Kids* shows kids ages 6 to 14 the fascinating truth about the world—and why they should care.
kids.nationalgeographic.com/subscribe

For information about special discounts for bulk purchases, please contact National Geographic Books Special Sales: specialsales@natgeo.com

For rights or permissions inquiries, please contact National Geographic Books Subsidiary Rights: bookrights@natgeo.com

Cover design by Amanda Larsen
Designed by Dawn Ripple McFadin

Hardcover ISBN: 978-1-4263-3326-2

The author and publisher gratefully acknowledge the expert review of pages 54–55 by Anton Treuer, Professor of Ojibwe at Bemidji State University, and the fact-checking of Sophie Massie.

Printed in China
18/RRDS/1